ADVENTURES IN SOUND
FOR PIANO

(For the Intermediate Level Student)

EMMA LOU DIEMER

Cover Design and Illustrations by Mark Linder

© 1989 Summy-Birchard Music
a division of Summy-Birchard Inc.
Secaucus, New Jersey, USA
All Rights Reserved   Printed in USA

ISBN 0-87487-662-1

Summy-Birchard Inc.
exclusively distributed by
Warner Bros. Publications Inc.
265 Secaucus Road
Secaucus, New Jersey 07096-2037

TABLE OF CONTENTS

ABOUT THE COMPOSER

EMMA LOU DIEMER began composing at the age of 7. By age 13, she had already written several piano concertos! She has written for orchestra, band, chamber ensembles, and choral groups as well as for the keyboard. Most of her music is published and much has also been recorded. She has won many composition awards including an annual ASCAP award, NEA and Ford Foundation grants and others.

Currently Professor of Composition at the University of California, Santa Barbara, and a keyboard performer on organ, synthesizer and piano, EMMA LOU DIEMER is a graduate of Yale and Eastman Schools of Music.

ABOUT "ADVENTURES IN SOUND"

These pieces were written for beginning and intermediate pianists and their teachers who either have a liking for and knowledge of contemporary music or who would benefit from learning more of the idioms and techniques for playing the piano that have been introduced and explored during this century.

The titles are descriptive of the moods and sounds in the various pieces. Four of the compositions use techniques other than traditional on-the-keys playing. The use of the damper pedal is carefully indicated and should be observed. The composer intended that this music be enjoyable as well as challenging!

ADVENTURES IN SOUND

FIST DANCE

Emma Lou Diemer

* The hands may need to be bent at the wrist to cover the notes. The chords may be played with fingers 1-2-3-4 instead.

** All metronome markings are approximate.

OVER AND OVER

Emma Lou Diemer

HAZY AFTERNOON

Emma Lou Diemer

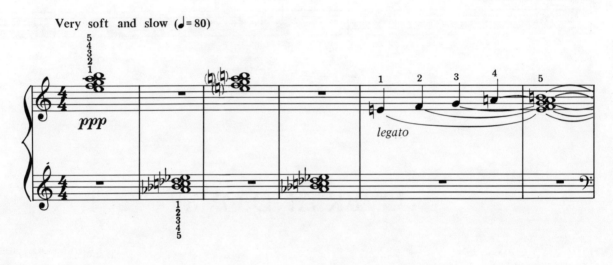

JAZZ ECHOES

Emma Lou Diemer

Lively, rhythmically (♩ = 132)

With the left arm, press silently as many of these white keys* as possible.
Do not use Pedal. (Hold cluster until the end of the piece).

* From C (two octaves below middle C) to F above middle C.

(hold down arm
until sound fades away)

THE GUITAR

Emma Lou Diemer

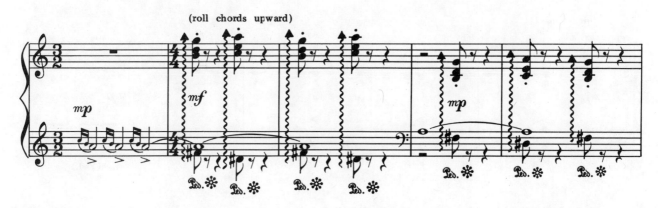

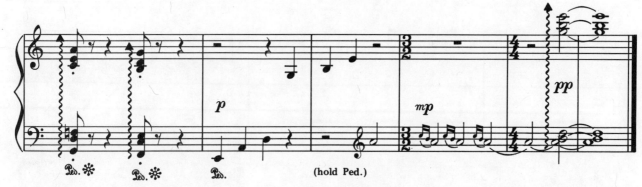

OLD SPANISH TOWN

Emma Lou Diemer

Moderately fast (♩ = 138)

Tap on bottom edge of music rack with fingers flat.

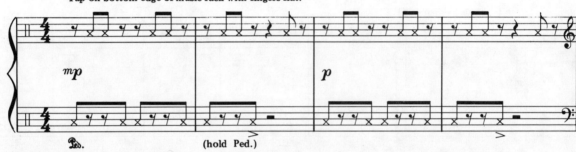

(on keyboard)

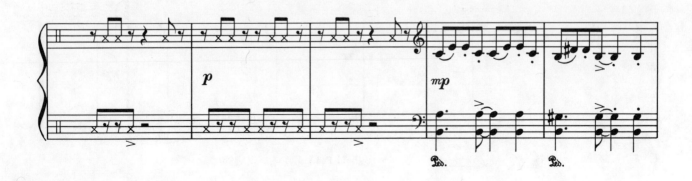

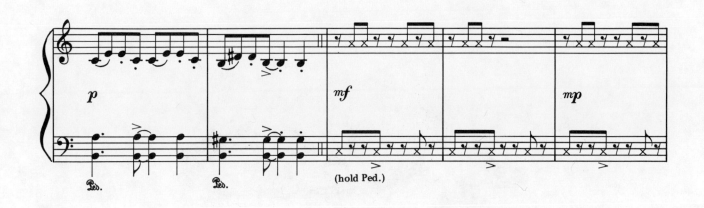

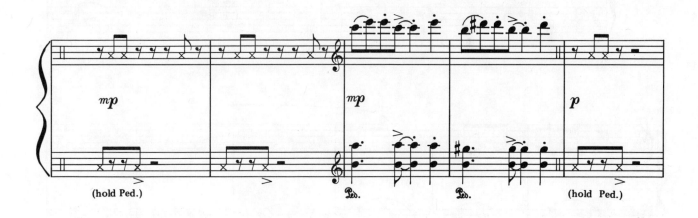

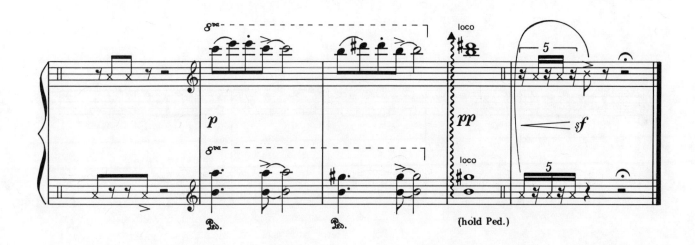

A RAINY SATURDAY

Emma Lou Diemer

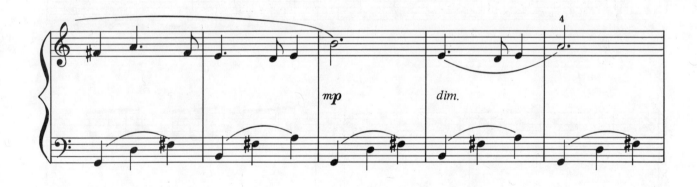

rit.

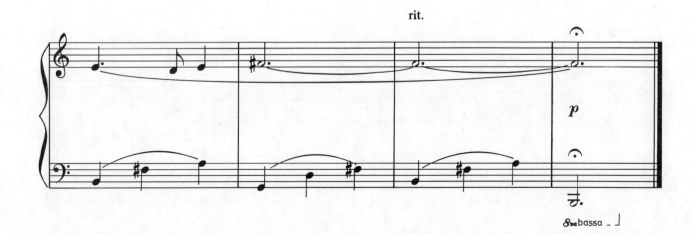

8va bassa

IN A HIGH STEEPLE

Emma Lou Diemer

Rather slow (♩= 76)
(*like bells*)

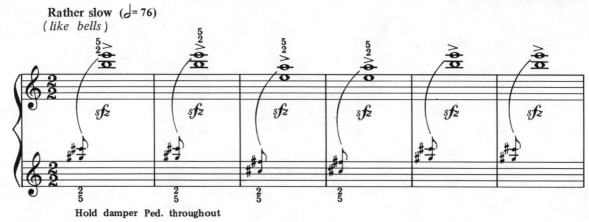

Hold damper Ped. throughout

legato

mf

rit.

a tempo

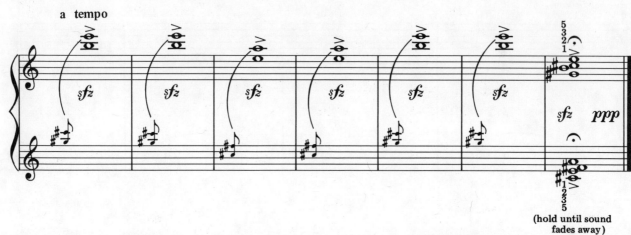

sfz *ppp*

(hold until sound
fades away)

IN A DEEP CAVE

Emma Lou Diemer

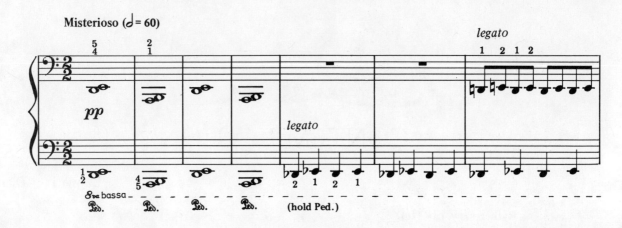

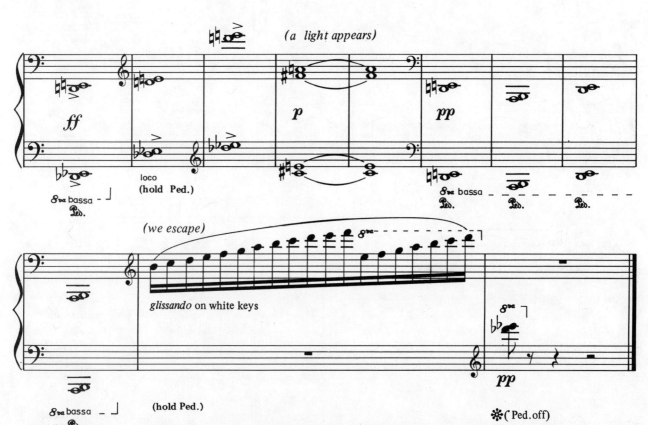

CONTEMPLATION

Emma Lou Diemer

GO FOURTH

Emma Lou Diemer

OUT OF AFRICA

Emma Lou Diemer

23

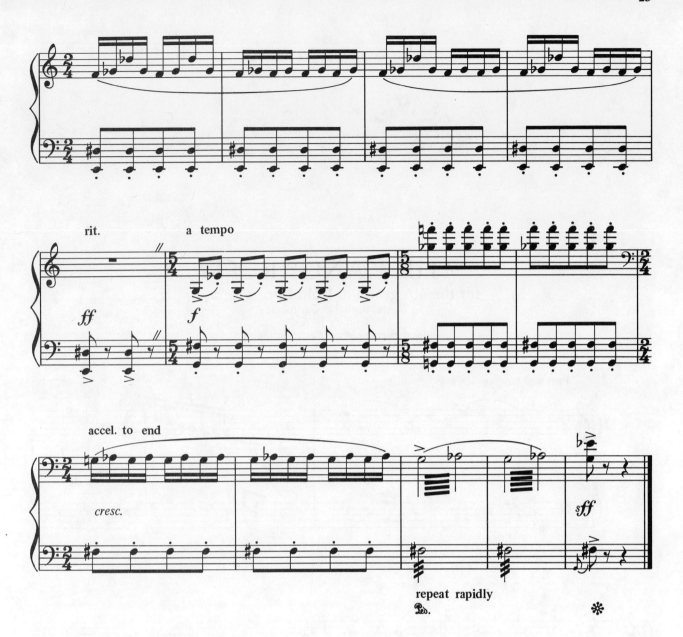

THE KANGAROO

for the 4th grade of Cold Spring School
Santa Barbara, California
January 1986
(and their teacher, Pete Shannon)

Emma Lou Diemer

EDITORIAL NOTES ABOUT "A HARP IN THE SKY"
AND "WIND IN THE WEST"

A. Both of the next two pieces require the player's DAMPING some of the strings of the piano. Piano strings must be easily accessible for damping. In general, "grand" pianos have accessible strings while most "upright" pianos do not. Therefore, we recommend that these pieces be played on grand pianos only.

In these two pieces, damping is achieved by pressing on the strings with the flat of the fingers. Therefore, to avoid damaging the sensitive parts of the piano, the following procedures should be applied:

1. RECEIVE CAREFUL GUIDANCE AND INSTRUCTION FROM THE TEACHER

2. THOROUGHLY WASH AND DRY HANDS AND FINGERS BEFORE STARTING

3. SLIDE THE MUSIC RACK ASSEMBLY BACK FROM THE KEYBOARD TO EXPOSE THE STRINGS FROM THE TUNING PINS TO THE DAMPERS.

Only certain strings are to be damped at any one time. The composer has indicated which strings are to be damped by using open rectangular bars which are located on the staff at the appropriate pitch locations. For example:

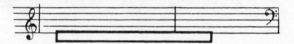

indicates that strings c', c♯', d', d♯' and e' are to be damped with the fingers of one hand.

B. The composer has indicated playing faster and slower in these pieces by using BEAMED ACCELERANDOS and RITARDANDOS as shown in the examples below:

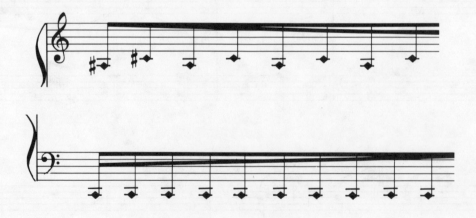

A HARP IN THE SKY

Emma Lou Diemer

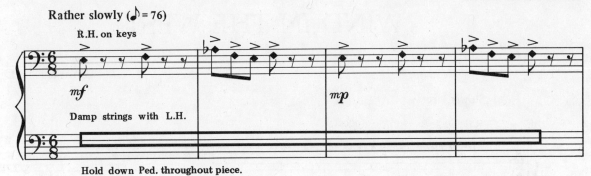

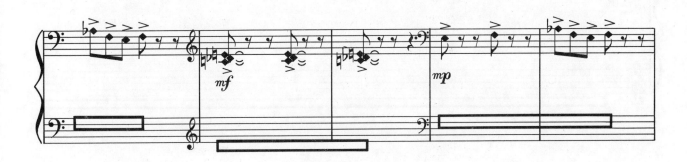

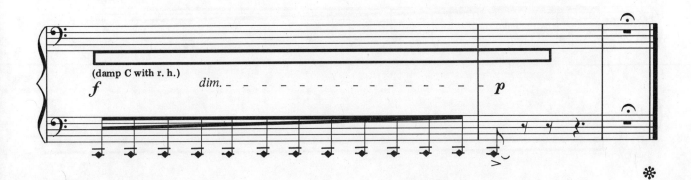

WIND IN THE WEST

Emma Lou Diemer

Slowly, freely

R.H. on keys   (accel.)

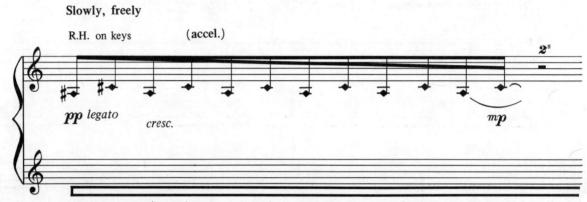

Damp only the A♯ and C♯ strings with L.H.. Hold down Ped. throughout piece.

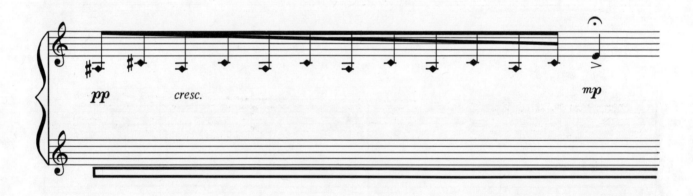

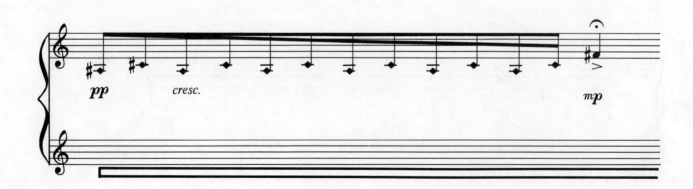

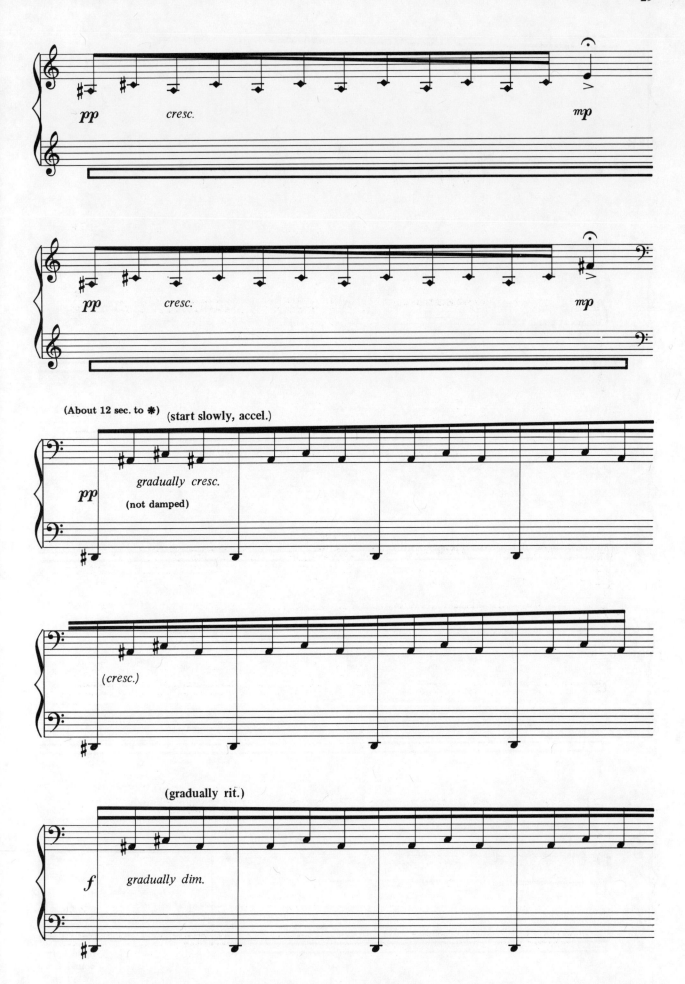